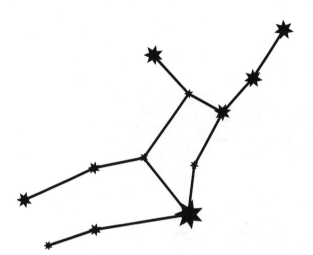

Ordering Information:
Quantity sales. Special discounts are available on quantity purchases by
corporations, associations, and others. For details, contact the "Special Sales
Department" at the following email address: hello@oneideapress.com.

Paperback Edition: 978-1-944134-61-7
Hardback Edition: 978-1-944134-62-4

Printed in the United States of America

Virgo

a love letter

Heidi Rose Robbins

with illustrations by
Wyoh Lee

hello love.

(yes, you)

Friends,

I'm so glad you are holding this book! It is filled with encouragement and an ongoing invitation for us all to be more fully who we are.

The best way to work with these books is to purchase one for each of your signs — your Sun, Moon, and Rising Sign.

These are the three most important positions in your astrological chart. You can discover what these are if you enter your exact time, date, and place of birth in any online astrology site. Each position has something unique to offer.

When you read the book for your Moon, think of it as an energy that is very available to you. It's a place where you might feel comfortable. The Moon has to do with our emotional life, our patterns of behavior, and circumstances of our childhood. We can rely on the Moon, but we also want to work to shed the patterns that no longer serve us.

The Sun is our present personality. We can learn a lot about our everyday self in the world. We can learn about the energies we have readily available to us to use in service to our highest calling.

The Rising Sign is the most important point. It is the sign that was rising as we took our first breath. It holds the key to our soul's calling. It is an energy we want to cultivate and be generous with throughout our lives.

So — enjoy the journey. Be sure to read them all!

Welcome
{13}

11

My dear Virgo,

This little book is a love letter to your intelligent, devoted self. It is written to remind you of your many gifts. It is written to be a loving mirror so any page can remind you who you truly are. Take it in, dear Virgo. I know you are sometimes very hard on yourself. But promise me you'll take the time to see your compassionate, and hard working self in these pages.

This little book will also explore those places in ourselves that start to close when we want to open, the part of us that hesitates when we want to act. We all have our quirks and difficulties, after all. But if we return again and again to our potency, vulnerability, and sense of possibility, we can outgrow our closures one by one.

Think of this book as a treasure chest containing the golden coins of YOU. Open it when you wish to remember your beauty, worth or great potential. And remember, too, this Virgo part of you is just one voice in the symphony of YOU. It cannot possibly contain your complexity and bounty. But it can begin to name just a few of your gifts.

Read this out loud when you can. Read this in the morning. Read it before bed. Read it when you need encouragement. Read it even if you are already feeling purposeful and clear. Let it fuel your work. But READ IT. And own it! And use it! And claim it! This is your love letter, Virgo. This is the song of YOU.

Big love,
Heidi Rose

Celebrating Virgo

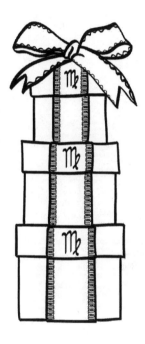

As you read this celebration, you will sometimes say "Yes, yes, yes! This is me!" And you may likewise sometimes feel that you have not yet lived into some of these qualities. This is honoring and celebrating the very best of your Virgo energy. This is naming the full, conscious, awakened use of your Virgo gifts. We are sounding the note of THE POSSIBLE. So, even if you feel you still have work to do in certain areas — as do we all — let these words be inspiration to offer your best Self!

♍

You bring the sacred
to the ordinary.

You understand how to bring
attention, care, and presence
to the most mundane of moments
or tasks, dear Virgo. You attend
to daily living with love
and devotion.

♍

You figure things out.

You never give up, dear Virgo.
When you reach an impasse, you
explore another route. You take
each problem or puzzle and give
your whole brilliant mind to its
unraveling.

♍

You are infinitely practical.

You are not easily swayed by emotion. You look at what needs to be done and take according action. You make lists. You act immediately. You get it done.

♍

You care deeply about physical, emotional, and mental health.

Health and wellness are incredibly important to you. You strive to be healthy on all levels. And you are very rigorous with yourself when it comes to achieving that state of health and wellness. You know how to help others improve their health as well and are always happy to serve as a guide.

♍

You devote yourself to whom
and what you love.

Though there is no sign quite as
practical as yours, there is also no
sign as devoted. You give yourself
wholly to those projects and people
you love. This is where
your intelligence marries your
depth of love.

♍

You have a keen analytical mind.

You are smart, smart, smart, dear Virgo. You have a clear, cool, investigative mind. When you are presented with data, you are not afraid to dive in and assess. In fact, you love it. You are seeking solutions and you find them.

♍

You know how to improve and
refine any project.

You have a meticulous eye for
detail. You know what needs to
be fixed. You see it immediately.
And you can present a clear
course of action to refine it.

♍

You are a great editor.

One of your super powers is your editorial eye. You catch the tiny imperfections that others do not. And you understand that one slight edit can make a world of difference.

♍

Your compassionate nature
takes practical action.

When you see someone who needs
help, you are not simply doing to
feel bad about it. You say,
"What can we do here? How can
we improve conditions?" Then,
you act.

♍

You make the best to-do lists.

You love your lists, dear Virgo.
They are clear and detailed.
They hold all your action items
and self-improvement steps.
And there is great satisfaction
is checking off each item,
isn't there?

♍

You know how to create a
system and execute a plan.

You are masterful at creating
flow, Virgo! You ask yourself, "What
is the best way to tackle this?"
You are the embodiment of the
efficient, well thought out action
that gets the job done.

♍

You attend to all the
minute details.

You see what most people do
not. You do not skip any steps.
You think things through with
precision, leaving no question
unasked, or no moment
unattended.

♍

You know how to practice.

You show up, Virgo! You practice whatever it is you have chosen to improve upon. It might be piano lessons or yoga, meditation or painting. You do nothing half way. If you say you want to learn something, you show up rhythmically to learn it!

♍

You build a sacred space for beauty and love to enter.

Whether in your home or place of business, you know how to create an exquisite space — aesthetically gorgeous and refined. You attend to the physical space with care and cleanliness so those who enter fell a sense of refinement and beauty.

♍

You are a source
of mother love.

You love through your physical
care and practical attention.
You attend to all the health
and wellness needs for those you
love, dear Virgo. You provide food,
blankets, doctor's appointments,
school supplies. You devote
yourself to others' well-being.

♍

You work hard.

You are the one to stay late at the office, to stick with the job until it is done. If you have assigned yourself a task, you will complete it no matter how long it takes. You want to be of service and you strive for perfection always. So, you are often working more than playing.

♍

You bring humility to all
you do.

You go about your work without a
lot of fanfare, Virgo. You are fast,
efficient, and productive. You
don't make a fuss. You are happy
to be of service. You are happy to
improve conditions.

♍

You know how to purify,
refine and improve health.

Did you know that Virgo rules the
intestines? You are excellent with
nutrition, Virgo! You know about
supplements and herbs. You know
about exercise and alternative
healing techniques. You inspire us
all to be more healthy.

♍

You love to be of service.

You love to be there to help get
the work done. You love to be
called upon for your expertise
and ability. And you have both.
There is something deeply
satisfying in a job well done.

♍

You have a quiet, meditative focus.

You observe quietly and with great attention. You see clearly and with precision. You work efficiently. You take care of things before anyone else has even noticed they need attention. You do your work with a quiet intensity.

You meet even the smallest needs.

You attend to the immediate need, no matter the size or scope. And you don't shy away from the less glamorous jobs. If someone needs to be fed, you feed them. If a room needs to be cleaned, you clean it. You see what needs to be done and you act.

Living Your Virgo Love

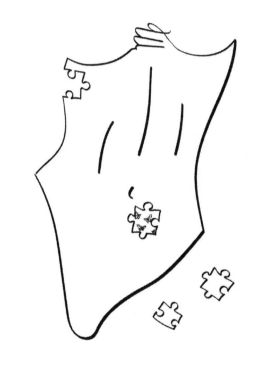

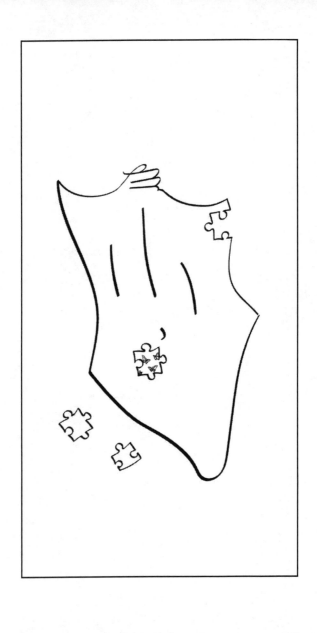

How are you feeling, dear Virgo? Can you sense the beauty and potency of your gifts? Do you want to make the very most of this devotional, precise energy of Virgo? Here are some thoughts about how to live fully into your Virgo love and how to nourish your Virgo spirit. Consider them little whispered reminders meant to help you THRIVE. Consider them 'action items' - a loving Virgo "to-do" list. Consider them invitations to live your most sacred life in your everyday callings.

♍

Volunteer.

You thrive when offering your
help, dear Virgo. Find something
that cracks your heart open
and show up to give your gifts.
You have an abundance
of information, care, and
practicality to offer.

♍

Share what you know about health and well-being.

You know more than most about physical, emotional, and mental health. Share what you know. Offer your nutrition tips or methods to combat anxiety. Share your list of healers. Circulate the latest health and wellness approaches.

♍

Help someone get organized.

You can organize and categorize
with your eyes closed, dear Virgo.
Step in, if you are so called,
and help another create more
flow in their life. Even a few
adjustments could make a world
of difference.

Do a deep dive researching
something you love.

Go ahead! Dive in. Learn a new
skill or research how to grow a
bio-dynamic garden. Find the
best way to do it. And then apply
yourself. You love discovering the
best methods and applications.

♍

Choose a practice.

What would you like to learn?
Do this for yourself, Virgo. Have
you always wanted to play the
guitar? The harp? Have you
always wanted a flourishing yoga
practice. Choose and begin your
practice. Give yourself this gift.

♍

Make a potion.

And by that I mean, make a fabulous health drink. Work with essential oils. Experiment with delicious and nutritious recipes. Make a signature cocktail. Have fun combining and stirring and testing and tasting.

♍

Experiment with how you eat.

Dear Virgo, you love to experiment with different ways of nourishing yourself. Go for it. You are very sensitive to what you put in and on your body. Experiment and see what works best.

♍

Make an altar.

Choose a place in your house
that you want to make a sacred
space. Make an altar that
captures a word or a feeling, or
calls in an energy you'd like to
cultivate. Sometimes we ourselves
can be walking altars. Wear a
necklace that has meaning.
Carry a prayer in your pocket.

♍

Help someone refine a creative offering.

Use your keen eye to help another create a masterpiece. Every artist needs some Virgo love to refine, package and produce. Lend your precision to a friend's creative offerings.

Growing Your Virgo Love

Sometimes, dear Virgo, we swing too far in one direction and need to invite a balancing energy to set us right. We are all growing and need to address the parts of ourselves that have not developed as fully. The opportunity for Virgo is to invite Pisces (your opposite sign) into the picture. Here are ways to grow your Virgo love to be more imaginative, compassionate and inclusive.

♍

Don't be so hard on yourself.

You demand a great deal of
yourself, Virgo. And you seek
perfection. The inner critic is
particularly strong. Try to be more
gentle with yourself.
Welcome self compassion.

♍

Don't be so hard on everyone else.

When we are intensely hard with ourselves, it's easy to look out into the world and see all the imperfections there as well. You will always notice what needs to be fixed, but try to soften your gaze and lead with love. Also, try to notice what IS working!

♍

Be patient with yourself
and others.

When you know how good
something can actually be, you
might drive yourself or others to
achieve a kind of perfection. Be
sure to let yourself and others
make mistakes and be human.

♍

Daydream.

Your to-do list is long. See if
you can add some time to
daydream. You need to gift
yourself with time to replenish,
dear Virgo. It's so easy for you
to over-work. Give yourself time
to rest.

♍

Listen to music.

Music often quiets the mind. And you have a powerful, analytical mind. Put on some music you love and sing along.

♍

End your work day when it is supposed to end.

Try not to over do. Experiment with leaving the office when you leave the office. And try to leave on time. Turn your attention to hearth, home, and nourishment when the work day is done.

♍

Be discriminating about
what is yours to do.

It's so easy to take on
EVERYTHING. But not
EVERYTHING is yours to do. Find
the things that make you feel
alive. Delegate what you can.
You are not here to work yourself
to the bone doing things that do
not nourish your Soul self.

Questions to Inspire
Sharing Your Virgo Love

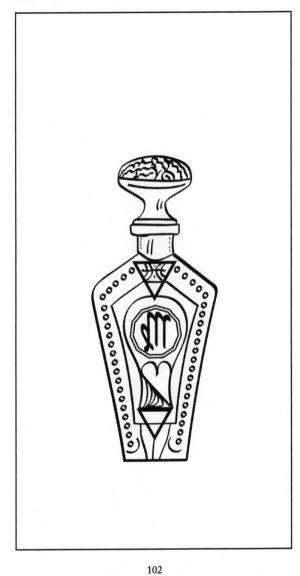

Dear Virgo, here are a few questions or prompts that might inspire or clarify your mission. Grab your journal. Write for 15 minutes about each. Don't edit. Dive in. Read your writing out loud or to a friend. Let this exploration spark your next purposeful action.

♍

This is the work
I love to do...

♍

If I could improve
anything in the world,
what would it be?

♍

When I work too hard I feel...

♍

I feel most critical of
myself and others when...

♍

Here's how it is,...

♍

Today I will be gentle with
myself in these ways...

♍

Praise something or someone
in the form of a poem or
a letter or a list.

♍

Here is a list (big and small)
of things I'd like to fix in my
life and in the world...

♍

This is what it feels like
to be healthy...

♍

Here are all the things
I love about the work I do...

One Last Little Love Note:

Virgo, I hope these questions and prompts spark new possibility in your life. You have so much to offer, so much to give. And your devotion and clarity inspire many. If you ever need a little encouragement, just dip into this little book for a reminder of your light.

Now go forth Virgo, and do your thing.

The World is Waiting for YOU.

Big love,
Heidi Rose

About the Author.

Heidi grew up with an astrologer father and an architect mother. Her father taught her the zodiac with her ABC's and her mother taught her to love art and appreciate the beauty of the natural world. She likes to call herself a poet with a map of the heavens in her pocket. Her passion is to inspire and encourage us all to be our truest, most authentic, radiant selves using the tools of astrology and poetry.

www.heidirose.com
Instagram @heidiroserobbins